T0130602

Saladin

LEVEL TWO 700 HEADWORDS

OXFORD
UNIVERSITY PRESS

Great Clarendon Street, Oxford OX2 6DP

Oxford University Press is a department of the University of Oxford.
It furthers the University's objective of excellence in research, scholarship,
and education by publishing worldwide in

Oxford New York

Auckland Cape Town Dar es Salaam Hong Kong Karachi
Kuala Lumpur Madrid Melbourne Mexico City Nairobi
New Delhi Shanghai Taipei Toronto

With offices in

Argentina Austria Brazil Chile Czech Republic France Greece
Guatemala Hungary Italy Japan Poland Portugal Singapore
South Korea Switzerland Thailand Turkey Ukraine Vietnam

OXFORD and OXFORD ENGLISH are registered trade marks of
Oxford University Press in the UK and in certain other countries

This edition © Oxford University Press 2010

The moral rights of the author have been asserted

Database right Oxford University Press (maker)

First published in Dominoes 2010

2014 2013 2012 2011 2010

10 9 8 7 6 5 4 3 2 1

ISBN: 978 0 19 424894 5 Book
ISBN: 978 0 19 424846 4 Book and MultiROM Pack
MultiROM not available separately

Printed in China

This book is printed on paper from certified and well-managed sources.

ACKNOWLEDGEMENTS

Illustrations and cover by: Jamel Akib

The publisher would like to thank the following for permission to reproduce photographs: Alamy
pp.22 (Wolfgang Kaehler), 23 (John Elk III), 30 (Roy Johnson/dbimages), 37 (Wolfgang
Kaehler), 54 (The Print Collector), 56 (c/Peter Horree), 57 (Ommayad Mosque/AWPhoto),
58 (Mary Evans Picture Library); Corbis pp.56 (a/Jon Arnold/JAI), 57 (Mehter band/Adam
Woolfitt), 57 (Mount of Olives/Antonio Barluzzi), 59 (Hoberman Collection), 60 (Napoleon
on Horseback at The St. Bernard Pass By Jacques-Louis David/Francis G. Mayer), 60 (George
Patton/Bettmann); Getty Images pp.56 (d/Jochen Schlenker/Robert Harding World Imagery),
56 (f/Daryl Benson/The Image Bank), 60 (Hannibal/Hulton Archive); The Kobal Collection
p.36 (Kingdom of Heaven/20th Century Fox); Photolibrary.com pp.14 (Vivienne Sharp/
Imagestate), 56 (e/Wojtek Buss/age fotostock), 57 (diving in the Red Sea/Armin Trutnau/
WaterFrame – Underwater Images), 60 (Julius Caesar/Riccardo Sala/Tips Italia); Rex Features
p.56 (b/J. Barry Peake)

DOMINOES

Series Editors: Bill Bowler and Sue Parminter

Saladin

Nina Prentice

Illustrated by Jamel Akib

Nina Prentice is a teacher who has worked in the Middle East and other countries. Because her mother is Italian, English is her second language. She remembers well how hard it was to spell in English when she first went to school, but it got much easier when she fell in love with reading. She likes going abroad to learn new languages and new ways of cooking. She now lives near Oxford, where she writes, goes walking and works in her garden.

OXFORD
UNIVERSITY PRESS

BEFORE READING

1 **The map shows important places in Saladin's life. Match the places with the explanations.**

a capital of Syria ☐ **d** capital of Palestine ☐

b capital of Egypt ☐ **e** old name for Istanbul ☐

c town where Saladin was born in 1138 ☐

2 **Choose the correct words to make sentences about the world in 1138.**

a The Emperor of the *Eastern/Western* church ruled in Byzantium.

b The Emperor of the *Eastern/Western* church ruled in Europe.

c People from *America/Europe* called 'Franks' were living in and ruling Palestine.

d Muslims of the time felt *happy/unhappy* that Jerusalem was in Frankish hands.

3 **Tick the correct sentence endings.**

People remember Saladin today because he…

a …was a famous fighter. ☐

b …was a good man. ☐

c …took Jerusalem from the Franks. ☐

d …was very rich. ☐

Chapter 1 – A small weak boy

Tikrit – 1138

'Help! Help! He's going to kill me!'

Hearing the screams, Shirkuh ran through the dark streets of the town. Suddenly he came around the corner of a building. A soldier was holding a knife to a woman's neck. Her eyes were wild and afraid. Shirkuh didn't stop to think. In a minute, the two men were fighting for the knife. In another minute, the soldier was dead, his blood bright red on the ground.

◇◇◇◇◇◇◇◇◇◇◇◇◇◇◇◇◇

Late that night, Ayyub heard a soft knock at the door. It was his brother Shirkuh asking for news.

'The baby hasn't come yet. The mother's having a bad time.' The father looked at his brother. 'Why are you hurrying?'

'Ayyub. I've just killed a man by mistake, but I was angry.'

'Shirkuh! Why did you do this? It'll be difficult for us here in Tikrit. The man's family will make trouble.'

'I couldn't stop myself. While I was coming home, a woman called out for help. A soldier was going to kill her. I didn't want to hurt him. It was an accident. But now **Governor** Zengi says that all our family must leave at once or we'll be in danger.'

'Oh, Shirkuh! You're a fighter. You're stronger than most men. But when you're angry, you stop thinking. It's always been this way, but I can't leave until the child arrives.'

Just then they heard a cry. Ayyub hurried away to the women's side of the house. 'What news?' he asked his sister.

'Good news, thank **God**! The child is born. But look at him. He's very small and **weak**. I don't think that he'll live through the night. The mother too is very ill,' she said.

'There's nothing to be done. We must go now!' Ayyub held his new son. 'I'll call you Yusuf because you must find a new life away from where you were born, like the **Prophet** Yusuf did in Egypt long, long ago.'

Baalbek – 1145

'Please, please tell us the story again! Please!' The three brothers were with their father, Ayyub, in the garden of his fine house in the old town. Turan Shah, the oldest boy, was next to his father. Yusuf, now seven years old, held Al-Adil, the baby, in his arms and sat as near as he could to listen.

Ayyub smiled and began:

*Six years before our Yusuf here was born, I was near the river Tigris catching some birds for your mother to cook for dinner. Suddenly, I saw a man on the other side of the water. He was having trouble running. He had blood all over his face and clothes, but he still carried his **sword**. Behind him I could see many soldiers riding fast horses. I thought quickly. Near me was a small fishing boat. I jumped in and pushed it across the river with a long stick.*

Just then, the soldiers started to get near the water. I called to the

2

man and helped him into the boat. I pushed the boat quickly into the river while the soldiers started shooting at us. **Arrows** hit the boat, but with God's help we weren't hurt! At last we got to the other side. Dirty, wet and tired, we ran back home. Your mother and sisters cooked us a wonderful meal that we enjoyed silently. The next morning I learned the name of my **guest**. It was the great Zengi himself! His army lost the **battle** the day before and all his soldiers were dead or prisoners. He wanted to hurry back to Mosul to make sure that the town was **safe** so I gave him new clothes and my best horse. Riding away, he said, 'I'll never forget your help and will always be a true friend to you and your family.'

'What was the horse like, Father?' asked Yusuf.

'All you think about is horses, Yusuf,' said Turan Shah.

'He was the brother of the wind. It's good to give with open hands. Zengi has been our friend since then. I'm Governor of Baalbek and we're safe and comfortable here because of him.'

arrow you shoot things with this

guest a person that you invite to your home

battle when two armies fight; to fight

safe not dangerous

polo a game like football where people ride horses and hit a ball with a stick

'Yusuf! You must come now. It's time to go to school.'

'Oh, Al-Adil, I don't want to go! Look at my horse, Aneed! I don't know why Turan Shah says that he's bad. He's going to be very good at **polo**. He always knows what to do!'

The boy of fourteen rode quickly up to the ball with the stick

in his hand. He hit it hard and sent it flying over to his brother. Al-Adil stopped the ball with his foot.

'Father says that you're the best rider of all of us, Yusuf. That's why, when Turan Shah couldn't do anything with Aneed, Father gave the horse to you. But you must go to school or you'll be in terrible trouble. Don't forget what Father said the last time that you were late!'

Yusuf jumped down from his horse's back and took him back to the house. Then he ran as fast as he could for school.

◇◇◇◇◇◇◇◇◇◇◇◇◇◇◇◇◇◇◇

The old teacher looked up angrily when Yusuf hurried into the room. He was very late. 'You'll have to stay this afternoon to do all the work that you've missed, boy!'

Yusuf sat next to Turan Shah. 'Where are we?' he asked.

Turan Shah showed Yusuf the words in the **holy Koran** that the boys were reading. 'It's the story of the Prophet Yusuf and how his brothers left him in the **desert** because they didn't like him,' he smiled, not very kindly.

'Stop talking and learn!' The teacher's stick hit both boys. It hurt. Turan Shah cried out, but Yusuf said nothing.

◇◇◇◇◇◇◇◇◇◇◇◇◇◇◇◇◇◇◇

'What am I going to do with you, Yusuf?' said his father later that day. 'Your teacher tells me that you're clever and quick to learn, but that you're never at school. I know that you're always with the horses, but you're not a child any more. You must learn to be a man and a soldier. I'm going to send you to my brother Shirkuh. You know that now he's an important **general** working for Zengi's son, Nuradin, up in Aleppo.'

'Can I take Aneed with me?'

'No! Since we came to Damascus you've only played. Now you must work. Get ready. We leave in an hour.'

holy belonging to God

Koran the Muslim holy book

desert a place that has no water

general a very important person in an army

5

READING CHECK

Match the people with what you find out about them in Chapter 1.

1 Shirkuh   **2** Ayyub   **3** General Zengi   **4** Yusuf   **5** Turan Shah

a He helps a man to escape from some enemy soldiers in a boat. ☑2

b He kills a soldier who is trying to kill a woman in the street. ☐

c He's got three sons. ☐

d He's born on the night that his family have to leave Tikrit. ☐

e He's a general in Aleppo. ☐

f He loves horses, and he isn't a very good student. ☐

g He's Ayyub's eldest son. ☐

h He's a very important man, and he gives Ayyub work. ☐

WORD WORK

1 Use the words to complete the sentences.

battle   guest   governor   weak   holy   safe

a The g̲o̲v̲e̲r̲n̲o̲r̲ of the city is one of my friends.

b Our soldiers won the .... after three days of fighting.

c We must find a .... place to hide the children.

d You must be my .... and stay the night at my home.

e The boy is very .... ; he needs food and rest.

f My parents want to visit Medina and other .... places next year.

2 Unjumble the letters to label the pictures.

DROWS	**WRAROS**	**LOOP**	**STERED**	**REALNEG**
1 ..sword..	2	3	4	5 ....

GUESS WHAT

What happens in the next chapter? Tick two boxes.

a Ayyub takes Yusuf to Aleppo to work with his Uncle Shirkuh. ☐

b Turan Shah goes to work as soldier with Nuradin's army ☐

c Nuradin and Yusuf are soon friends, and they play polo together. ☐

d Shirkuh says kind things to Yusuf, and helps him. ☐

Chapter 2 – A chance to prove himself

Aleppo, Syria – 1152

Yusuf felt sad saying goodbye to his mother and sisters before he left Damascus with his father. At first he was excited to be starting a new life, but after four days of hard travel on hot dry roads, he was worried. He asked himself over and over again, 'Will I be a good soldier?'

'Yusuf, look! That's where you'll live,' his father said while they rode through some small villages just outside Aleppo.

On a high hill in the middle of the town, the boy saw the tall walls of the **castle** climb up towards the sky. They made Yusuf feel very small and unimportant. The building looked like it was growing even taller while he rode through the town towards it. Yusuf wanted to go back home, but he knew that he couldn't say anything to his father. Ayyub rode up into the castle and Yusuf followed silently. They found the general talking to his men in a large room full of swords. Shirkuh was an **ugly** man, with only one eye. No one could say that he looked like a general, but he was **brave** and he knew everything about the best ways to fight and win.

After the soldiers left, the general turned to the boy.

'Well, Yusuf, are you sure that you want to be a soldier?'

'I'll do my best, Uncle.'

'If you want to be one of my soldiers, you'll do what I tell you. Do you understand?'

'Yes, Uncle.'

Shirkuh now turned to his brother.

'Ayyub, I'll take the boy, but only because you and I are brothers. I don't think that he'll be a good fighter or a soldier, but we'll see. If he's any trouble, he goes home – at once!'

Yusuf wanted to do well, but it was difficult. He tried hard to

castle a large building with strong, high walls

ugly not beautiful

brave not afraid of doing dangerous things

learn. But he was still small and weak and he found the fighting hard. His sword was heavy. The other soldiers were fast and strong. His uncle was often angry.

'Hey, Yusuf! You'll never be a soldier if you fight like that! I can't use you as you are. Go and try to understand how the **law** works from Governor Nuradin. I don't want to see you here again until you can do something better than this! Work hard or you'll go back home.'

Yusuf did what his uncle said. He thought, 'I'll never be a soldier. What will my father say if I have to go home? Learning the law is so boring, but Uncle Shirkuh thinks I can't do anything else. Oh, I want to be strong like other boys!'

Now he stood for long hours in the governor's rooms in the castle watching people asking Nuradin for help. At first everything was hard to understand, but soon Yusuf saw that Nuradin was a great man. The governor always listened to everybody – poor people, and women and children, too – not

law something that tells you what you must or must not do

just rich and strong men. The governor studied the law and talked about difficult **problems** with **wise** men. He thought about their words and took time to find the right answer.

After three months, the governor saw that Yusuf learned quickly. People liked the boy because he was friendly to everyone. His thin face usually looked sad when he was alone, but when he spoke to people, he had a kind and happy smile. He also always tried to help anyone with troubles. Nuradin began to talk to the boy about the problems of the castle, the town and the army. The governor also talked to Yusuf about his great hope:

'One day soon I want to make all the **Muslim** people stop fighting each other. We must work together to take Jerusalem back from the **Franks**. Palestine isn't their **land** after all. Nothing is more important than this, and we must all fight to make it happen!'

Now Yusuf wanted to fight the Franks too. It was wrong that they held the holy places. He also understood that Franks sometimes made friends with some Muslims and together they fought against other Muslims and took their houses, land and animals. Nothing was safe. It was also very hard for Muslims to go on **pilgrimage** to the holy city of Makkah. The road was too dangerous because of all the Frankish castles near it.

'I must get into Nuradin's army! But how can I do it when Uncle Shirkuh thinks that I'm too weak? I'll have to learn clever ways to win against stronger men. I know that the Franks are good fighters. Their horses are bigger, their soldiers wear a lot of **armour**, and they have many castles. But I know that we'll win if we work together and make good plans.'

From that day, he borrowed a horse and learned to use his sword day and night when he wasn't working for Nuradin. He

problem something difficult

wise intelligent, clever

Muslim a person who follows the religion of Islam, and the teachings of the Prophet Mohammed

Frank a person from Europe who lived in Palestine between 1099 and 1291

land country

pilgrimage a special journey to a religious place

armour a metal suit that soldiers wore in the past to stop people killing them

wanted to show his uncle that he wasn't just a good student of law, but also a real soldier.

One day, Nuradin asked Yusuf to play polo with him. The boy ran to find a horse. He was so excited, and he forgot about everything – his uncle, the law, and even fighting the Franks! They played inside the castle walls. Everyone watched Yusuf and his horse following the ball closely, without a mistake.

Polo was like a battle, fast and dangerous. Many horses fell, men were hurt, and one died when a horse ran over him, but Yusuf rode wonderfully. He stayed out of trouble and, by hitting clever shots, he helped Nuradin and his players to win.

'How can you play polo so well?' the governor asked the boy.

'I learned it in Damascus, sir. I have a wonderful horse there. My father says that he'll send him to me when General Shirkuh says that I can fight with the army.'

'Tell your father to send the horse now. You're small and not very strong, but you're a clever fighter. You think before you do things, and you want to win. There's nothing more important in a soldier. The general will be happy to have another good man in his army. Go to him now and tell him what I said.'

The general looked up when he heard the news. He wasn't smiling. 'Very well. You can come back, but don't think that you'll be fighting. Polo and **war** are different. You'll work in my office and learn how to move fighting men and horses quickly and to find food, **weapons**, and a safe place for them to sleep. Remember that brave soldiers and fast horses are only half the story. We only win wars when strong men are ready to fight in the right place at the right time.'

Yusuf was in the army now, but life wasn't easier. Every day he made sure that the soldiers and their horses had good food to eat. He counted weapons and made sure that they were strong and **clean**. He paid soldiers and kept the army's money safe. He found answers to all kinds of problems from morning until night, but sometimes he felt sad because he never knew if his uncle was happy with his hard work. There was no fighting for Yusuf, but sometimes Nuradin asked him to play polo and on Aneed's back he forgot his troubles.

war fighting between countries

weapon a thing that you use for fighting

clean to stop something being dirty

Aleppo – 1163

Yusuf was twenty-five, and still working for his uncle, when news came of trouble in Egypt. **Vizier** Shawar wanted Nuradin's help to keep the country out of the hands of his enemies. He **promised** to give a lot of money to the Syrians to make them come, but it was only when Amalric, the Frankish King of Jerusalem, decided to move into Egypt that Nuradin began to think about sending his army. 'The Franks mustn't get to Cairo and use the money that they find there to make their armies in the Holy Land stronger,' he said.

Yusuf worked hard for months to get the soldiers ready for the long journey to Egypt. There was a lot to do and General Shirkuh was always busy. He spoke to Yusuf only to give him more work and more difficult problems to put right. The young man worried that he couldn't go on the **campaign**, but he worked as hard as possible to make ready all that the army needed. The days went by and still Yusuf heard nothing about going. He knew that the army was leaving in less than a week.

'My uncle will leave me behind, and I'll spend the rest of my life counting swords and paying soldiers!' he thought sadly.

vizier an important man in the Muslim world; he helped a king take care of a country

promise to say that you will certainly do something

campaign a plan for an army to win battles or a war

READING CHECK

Choose the correct words to complete the sentences.

a Yusuf is ~~excited about~~/ afraid of what he must do as a soldier in Aleppo.

b Shirkuh sends Yusuf to learn about law / to be a soldier with Governor Nuradin.

c Yusuf works hard, and Shirkuh / Nuradin is happy with him.

d Nuradin talks about the Franks in Jerusalem, and Yusuf wants to help / fight them.

e Nuradin tells Yusuf to send for his horse / father, and to fight with Shirkuh's army.

f Shirkuh feels angry / happy having Yusuf with him, and he stops him from fighting.

g Syria / Egypt has problems with the Franks, and Nuradin decides to send his army to fight there.

h Yusuf organizes the army / the boats for the journey, but he isn't sure if he will go.

WORD WORK

1 Circle 12 more new words from Chapter 2 in the wordsquare.

P	I	L	G	R	I	M	A	G	E	R	C
R	D	E	B	A	S	E	W	U	M	L	A
O	N	W	E	A	P	O	N	S	N	E	S
M	R	A	B	R	E	K	A	H	F	A	T
I	L	R	S	M	U	S	L	I	M	S	L
S	E	L	P	O	U	B	O	T	O	R	E
E	C	A	Q	U	B	R	F	A	E	I	S
G	U	I	O	R	C	A	P	G	N	K	A
F	R	A	N	K	S	V	I	Z	I	E	R
L	I	N	H	A	P	E	L	E	N	D	T
A	H	J	T	C	A	M	P	A	I	G	N
W	I	S	E	M	J	Q	E	P	G	U	O

2 Complete the sentences about the story with the words from the wordsquare.

a In Aleppo Yusuf goes to live in Nuradin's c a s t l e.

b It's dangerous to make the _ _ _ _ _ _ _ _ _ _ to Makkah.

c The _ _ _ _ _ _ of Egypt asks Nuradin for help.

d Yusuf doesn't want the _ _ _ _ _ _ to be in Palestine.

e Yusuf helps his uncle to plan the _ _ _ _ _ _ _ _ in Egypt.

f Shirkuh looks strange, but he's a _ _ _ _ _ general.

g The Frankish soldiers wear a lot of _ _ _ _ _ _ _.

h The Egyptians _ _ _ _ _ _ _ _ to give money to the Syrians if they help them.

i The Syrians are getting ready to fight a _ _ _ in Egypt.

j Nuradin, Shirkuh, and Yusuf are all _ _ _ _ _ _ _ _.

k Yusuf understands that Nuradin is a _ _ _ _ man.

l Shirkuh tells Yusuf to study _ _ _.

m Yusuf helps to get _ _ _ _ _ _ _ for Shirkuh's soldiers.

GUESS WHAT

Who does what in the next chapter?

Yusuf

Vizier Shawar

Amalric, the Frankish King

Shirkuh

a They go to Egypt together.

....

b They fight together against the Franks.

....

c He doesn't pay the gold that he promised at first.

....

d He helps the Egyptians fight against the Syrians.

....

e He helps to keep the people of Alexandria safe.

....

f He feels angry with the Egyptian vizier.

....

Chapter 3 – The fight for Egypt

Egypt – 1164

'What are you doing, Yusuf? Why aren't you ready to go?' Shirkuh's face was red and angry.

Yusuf jumped up when his uncle came into his office in the castle of Aleppo. 'Why, Uncle, do you want me on the campaign? You said nothing about me coming, so I thought that you wanted me to stay here to take care of things.'

'Stupid boy! You know everything about my soldiers now. I need you to make sure that they have everything they need. Go! We leave tomorrow at first light!'

It didn't take long for Yusuf to find his sword, a few clothes and his holy Koran, and then to get his horse ready. At last he was one of Nuradin's soldiers, and not just an office boy for his uncle. 'If I do well in Egypt, perhaps one day I can be in the army that will take back the holy places!' he thought.

'Men!' Shirkuh called, 'To take our enemies by surprise, we must move quickly. The journey will be very difficult, but never forget that you're the best soldiers in Syria. We'll do good work for Nuradin in Egypt, and then the people and the gold of that rich country will help us to fight the Franks in the Holy Land.'

There was a great shout from the men. Then they all jumped on their horses and rode out through the castle gates. While he followed the general and his men, Yusuf thought, 'No one will ever see me afraid! I'll do my very best and, with God's help, my uncle, my father and Nuradin will see that I have done well!'

The road was long and hard, but Yusuf worked without stopping to help Shirkuh get the army safely to Egypt. It was important that all the men, their weapons, and their horses were ready for the fight once they arrived.

Yusuf enjoyed the campaign. Best of all was fighting at Shirkuh's side, riding with the Syrian army against King Amalric and his Frankish **knights,** and against the Egyptian enemies of Vizier Shawar. Yusuf watched and learned while his uncle won quickly with a few short, well-fought battles.

With the help of the Syrians, Shawar was soon the strongest man in Egypt once again. But he wanted to be strong without the help of Nuradin's army, and he did not want to pay Nuradin the gold that he promised him before. Shawar decided to talk to the Franks. 'I don't like General Shirkuh and the Syrians. They want to get their hands on Egypt, so I want your knights to push him and his army out of the country. If you do what I ask, I'll give you the money that I promised Nuradin!'

The Frankish generals agreed to help Shawar, and they battled against Shirkuh and his soldiers and pushed them out of Egypt. The Syrians fought bravely, but in the end they had to go back to Aleppo with nothing to show for their hard work. Nuradin was very angry. He thought that the campaign was a bad use of time, money, horses and men. He didn't want his army to go to Egypt ever again. Shirkuh was angry too.

'Don't worry, Yusuf,' he said to his **nephew**, 'Shawar will never win against me! Just wait. Nuradin doesn't want more fighting now, but when he sees how Amalric and the Franks get rich in Egypt with Shawar's help, he'll send us again. And then we'll make that criminal Shawar sorry that he was ever born!'

Egypt –1167

The old general was right. Three years later, Yusuf, now twenty-nine, was **marching** beside his uncle at the head of the Syrian army. 'Why aren't we taking the same road to Egypt as last time, General?' asked Yusuf.

'Shawar and the Franks know that we're coming. We must

knight a Frankish soldier usually from a good family

nephew your brother's (or sister's) son

march when soldiers walk into battle

travel quickly and secretly. My hope is to surprise them by taking the road down to the Dead Sea, and then travelling through the Sinai Desert. We'll get into the country by the back door while our enemies are looking for us through their front windows!'

'But, Uncle, won't it be terrible for the men?'

'Yes, but my soldiers are brave, and they want to win against Shawar and his Frankish friends. They'll do it!'

They crossed the hot dry land and near Suez, there was a deadly desert storm that very nearly killed them all. Men and horses were ill or died, but Yusuf spoke to the soldiers to help them go on bravely: 'Nuradin needs you to teach Shawar that he can't break his promises to Syrians and stay out of danger! Under Shirkuh we'll have a great **victory** in Egypt and then he'll give rich presents for the bravest!'

Finally, they arrived. The men were very weak, and Shirkuh decided that they weren't ready to fight against the large armies of Vizier Shawar and King Amalric. He stopped his soldiers at Giza, on the other side of the river from Cairo.

victory winning a fight

'We'll wait and see what they do. I know that Shawar's in trouble. Most Egyptians don't like it that he's friendly with the Franks. Everyone hates it when he gives Egyptian money to Amalric because they know that he uses it to keep the Franks fighting in the Holy Land. No Muslim wants this! Before long, all the Egyptians will fight for us.'

At last, early one spring morning, Yusuf ran to his uncle. 'Sir, the enemy's coming!'

The old general looked at his nephew. 'Today, I want you to do some real fighting, Yusuf. Take the group of soldiers in the middle of my army. Make the Frankish knights think that you and your men are weak and afraid. Turn and run. They'll follow with the hope of killing many of you, but I'll take the rest of our army around them. Then you'll surprise them when you turn round and fight!'

Yusuf was worried, 'Will I do well? Will the men follow me and do what I ask?' But there were no problems. The plan worked! King Amalric was lucky to get away safely, but Syrian swords and arrows killed many of his knights. It was a great victory for Nuradin's men, but Shirkuh knew that he was not safe.

'Yusuf, you're a good soldier, and one day I know you'll be a great general. But we can't stop now. Take the men to Alexandria where we have friends. I'll get the country people to help me make trouble for Shawar and the Franks here. I'll come and help you when I've finished.'

◇◇◇◇◇◇◇◇◇◇◇◇◇◇◇◇◇◇◇◇

It was a long time before Yusuf and his men saw the general again. For months Yusuf and his small army fought to keep Alexandria safe from the Franks. The enemy came by land and by sea. No food or help could come into the town from outside and **siege engines** sent stones and dead animals over the **city** walls. This made life terrible for the people and the soldiers inside the city. Many were ill, all were hungry, and many died. But Yusuf kept his men fighting, while he worked as hard as possible to make the lives of the people of Alexandria easier.

siege engine something that armies used in the past to break down the walls of castles or towns that they were attacking

city (*plural* **cities**) a big and important town

'I'm sorry!' he said, 'It's because you're our friends that you're in trouble now. But I know that my uncle will come soon and then the **siege** will be over. Until he arrives, be strong and brave! I promise that the enemy won't take the town while we're here, and my men and I will do all that we can to keep you safe.'

Yusuf was right. At last his uncle came with his new army and ended the siege. The town was out of danger, but the war wasn't over yet. And there was a lot of work to do to make the people of Alexandria truly safe. Yusuf went to talk to the Franks to try to find ways to help the sick and **wounded** Muslims in the town. 'Will the Franks understand that it's wrong to fight old men, women, and children?' he worried. 'I must remember all that I learned from Nuradin about talking to angry and difficult people. If I'm wise and careful, God will help me.'

After the long siege, Amalric's men already knew that Yusuf was a good soldier. While he explained the problems of the people of Alexandria, the Franks learned that he was a good man, too. Humphrey of Toron, an important knight, said, 'General Shirkuh's nephew, Yusuf, is more truly **chivalrous** than any of us! I **wish** that we worried as much as he does about those that are too weak or sick to fight. I'd like to make him a knight, even if he's a Muslim.' It was from this time that people in Europe began to hear how kind and **generous** Yusuf was.

While Yusuf tried to make things better in Alexandria, Vizier Shawar gave the Syrians gold to make them leave Egypt, but Shirkuh was still angry. He wanted to win the war and he wanted the Franks out of the country. Most of all, he wanted Shawar out of Cairo, and he thought that most Egyptians wanted this too. But Yusuf, after his terrible time in Alexandria, was happy to march back home.

siege when an enemy army waits around a castle or town and attacks it until the people inside open the doors to them

wounded hurt

chivalrous how a knight should be: kind and ready to help old people, women and children

wish to want something very much

generous always ready to give things to other people

READING CHECK

Are these sentences true or false? Tick the boxes.

		True	False
a	Shirkuh tells Yusuf to go with him to Egypt.	☑	☐
b	Nuradin himself goes to Egypt to make sure that the Egyptians will help fight against the Franks in Palestine.	☐	☐
c	The Syrian soldiers help Shawar to win the war against the Franks.	☐	☐
d	Shawar doesn't want to pay Nuradin, so he asks the Franks to help him.	☐	☐
e	The Syrians win the battle and then return to Aleppo.	☐	☐
f	Three years later the Syrian soldiers return to fight again in Egypt.	☐	☐
g	They cross the desert easily.	☐	☐
h	Yusuf goes with a big army to fight for Alexandria.	☐	☐
i	The Franks think that Yusuf is a good soldier, and a good person too.	☐	☐
j	At last Shawar gives Shirkuh gold to make sure that the Syrians leave Egypt.	☐	☐
k	Yusuf is happy to return to Syria, but his uncle still wants to fight Shawar.	☐	☐

ACTIVITIES

WORD WORK

Use the words in the siege engine to complete the diary of one of Yusuf's soldiers.

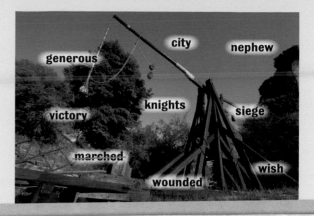

Alexandria

We **a)** .marched.. here across the desert with General Shirkuh's
b) .... , Yusuf. He's a kind and **c)** .... man,
and on the way, he helped many poor Egyptians.

When we arrived here in the **d)** .... of Alexandria, the
people were happy to see us, but Amalric and his Frankish
e) .... soon came. Now, because of their **f)** .... ,
we have little food or water. There are many **g)** .... and
sick people here in Alexandria, and we're trying to help them.
I **h)** .... that we had some more water and good food for
them. When Shirkuh arrives with his army, we're sure that we'll
have a great **i)** .... , and we'll make the Franks leave.

GUESS WHAT

What happens in the next chapter? Tick three boxes.

a Shirkuh and Yusuf go to Egypt for a third time. ☐
b Amalric and his knights help the Egyptian people. ☐
c Yusuf becomes the new Vizier of Egypt. ☐
d Yusuf changes his name to Saladin. ☐
e Nuradin is happy with Yusuf's work in Egypt. ☐
f Yusuf goes back to Syria to fight Nuradin. ☐

23

Egypt – 1168

The people hiding in their houses heard the sound of horses and men in armour first. Then the screams and cries began. Outside in the narrow streets of Bilbais, everyone was trying to run away from danger, but it was hopeless. Amalric's knights on their war horses were everywhere. Their bright swords were red with the blood, not just of the soldiers fighting them, but of the people in the town too. No one was safe, and at the end of that terrible day, the streets were silent and bloody.

After the Franks killed so many people near Cairo, **Caliph** Al-Adid sent a secret letter to Nuradin. He wrote:

> *I no longer think that Vizier Shawar is **loyal** to the Egyptians. He is too friendly with the Franks, and all the money that Shawar pays to King Amalric does nothing to stop Amalric's knights killing my people. They want all the country. Then, when they have it, they'll use all our gold to make their castles and armies even stronger. Shawar's ready to give them anything as long as he can be the strongest man in Egypt. We're all in great danger. Please help us!*

Nuradin called Yusuf and said, 'Find General Shirkuh.'

Yusuf went to the old general sadly. When his uncle told him to get ready for another campaign in Egypt, Yusuf said, 'By God! Even if you give me the whole country, I won't go!' He still remembered the terrible siege of Alexandria. But Nuradin's **orders** were law to all his men. So in a few short days, the army was on its way to Egypt for the third time. Early in January 1169, after three weeks' journey, they marched into Cairo. Everyone was happy to see the Syrians. The Franks left the country without a fight, and the Egyptians felt safe at last. The Caliph said, 'Shawar is a criminal. He was loyal only to himself, not to Egypt or to me, and now he must die. You must kill him, Yusuf.'

With Shawar's death, Shirkuh was the new vizier. He gave all the beautiful things in Shawar's house to the people of Cairo. He was also now the **commander** of the Egyptian army, but his love of food killed him after only two months. One day, halfway through a wonderful meal, he gave a great cry and died.

Important men working for the Caliph asked, 'Who will be the new vizier? We must find a good man.'

Caliph a very important religious man in an Arab country

loyal a person who is loyal does not change his friends

orders words that tell somebody to do something

commander the most important person who tells soldiers what to do

pray to talk to
God

organize to
make something
work well

'We also need a new commander,' the Syrian generals said.

It was difficult. The Egyptians wanted one of their people as vizier and commander of their army, and Nuradin's men couldn't work for someone from anywhere but Syria.

'I know,' said someone, 'Let's make Yusuf the new vizier. He's only thirty, and knows nothing about ruling a country. We'll tell him what to do, and he'll do it!' Many agreed that Yusuf was the right man for the job, and so he became both vizier of Egypt and commander of the Syrian and Egyptian armies.

Not everyone was happy to see Yusuf in this important job. A few soldiers went to Syria to tell Nuradin that the new vizier, Yusuf, wanted to take over Egypt. Nuradin was angry. So, to show that he was loyal to his old commander, Yusuf went with the Caliph and the people to **pray** for Nuradin every Friday.

When his brother Turan Shah arrived from Syria, Yusuf told him, 'It's not easy here but, thank God, I learned the law from Nuradin, and how to **organize** armies from my uncle because we have enemies everywhere – not just the Franks!'

Yusuf was right. One day, one of his soldiers saw that one of the Caliph's men was wearing very strange shoes on his feet when he left the Caliph's great house. Inside one of these shoes was a secret letter which Yusuf opened and read.

The Egyptians wanted Amalric and his knights to **attack** Yusuf and the Syrians, but the Franks never saw that letter. In the end the Franks came, but Yusuf and his army were ready for them, and sent them away again without any problems.

attack to start fighting

religion how people think about God and pray to Him

Yusuf was a careful ruler, and Egypt quickly grew into a strong country under him. He decided that it was wrong to have a rich life, and that it was more important to help people in trouble. So he took a new name, Saladin, which means 'the good of **religion**', to show that he wanted to be a good Muslim. And he gave all the expensive presents that people gave him to the Egyptians and to his soldiers. He lived in a small house, and used his money as a vizier to build schools and hospitals. He also made the walls of Cairo stronger, and built a great castle on the Muqattam hills. 'I want the Egyptian people to know that we are on their side, and that we want their country to be strong and safe. Then they will be happy to fight with us against the Franks,' he told his Syrian generals.

But Nuradin was more and more angry. He wrote:

> *Yusuf – I'm your commander! You're spending all your time ruling a country that doesn't belong to you. You're getting strong and rich with Egypt's gold, but I want you, your new soldiers, and the money that you've won with me, here, to fight the Franks in the Holy Land. Unless you come back to Syria immediately, I'll attack you!*

Some young men in Saladin's army said, 'If the King of Syria comes here, we'll fight him and send him back to his country!'

But Ayyub, Saladin's father, told him, 'I'll kill you myself if you go against your commander!' Saladin listened and waited.

In 1174, Nuradin died. His last words were, 'Only one thing makes me unhappy: what will happen to my family at the hands of Yusuf, son of Ayyub?'

Because Nuradin's son, Al-Saleh, was only eleven years old, many people wanted to **rule** Syria in the boy's name. Then two months later, King Amalric of Jerusalem died too. His son, Baldwin, was thirteen, and was ill with **leprosy**. Saladin, now thirty-six, saw that it was a good time to move against the Franks, but he needed a bigger army.

'If I can teach Nuradin's son how to be a good ruler while he's still young, and I can rule Syria in his name, then all Muslims will help my soldiers fight for the Holy Land,' he thought.

But many Syrians were afraid of Saladin. The **emirs** said, 'You go too far, Yusuf! You were just a soldier, and now you want all of Syria! You came from nothing. You are nothing. And we won't listen to you!'

But Saladin wanted to make Nuradin's dream of winning back the Holy Land come true. He took Damascus with little trouble. Then he moved on to Aleppo. This was where the young Al-Saleh went with his emirs after they saw how quickly Saladin was winning the country. But Aleppo was difficult to take, so Saladin attacked the castle of Azaz first. It fell after thirty-eight days of fighting, and then Aleppo **surrendered**.

The emirs didn't **trust** Saladin and thought that he really wanted to be King of Syria, so they asked the Assassins, a secret group of killers, to kill him. They tried twice, while Saladin was asleep, but he was lucky and lived. He decided to fight the Assassins in their mountain home, but it wasn't easy. Some of his soldiers said, 'We were near Sinan, the Assassins' general, but he has great **powers** that we can't explain. He looked at us, and we couldn't lift our swords to fight him!'

rule to decide what happens in a country; when you decide what happens in a country

leprosy this illness makes people very ill and changes the way they look and, in the past, it killed them

emir a ruler or commander of a group of people or part of a Muslim country

surrender to stop fighting because you cannot win

trust to believe that someone is on your side

power something that makes you strong

One night Saladin made a **trap** to catch anyone trying to get near him while he was sleeping. In the morning he found some sweet bread near his head. A knife through it held a message saying: *You are under our power!* No one could explain how the things got there.

'Perhaps Sinan does have special powers!' thought Saladin, 'We must stop fighting him and his people.'

No one knew what Saladin and Sinan agreed, but the Assassins never tried to hurt Saladin again. By 1177, most of Syria wanted to help Saladin, who was now thirty-nine. Then the news came that the Franks and the people in Byzantium were no longer friends. Saladin felt that perhaps now was the time to start a holy war to take Jerusalem back from the Franks.

trap something that is made to catch an animal or person

READING CHECK

Order the sentences to summarize Chapter 4.

a Nuradin and Amalric both die in the same year. ☐

b The emirs ask the Assassins to kill Saladin. ☐

c After Shirkuh dies, Yusuf is made Vizier of Egypt. ☐

d Nuradin sends Shirkuh and the army back to Egpyt. ☐

e Nuradin wants Saladin to go back to Syria with money and men to fight against the Franks. ☐

f Saladin talks to Sinan, the general of the Assassins, and they agree not to fight. ☐

g Saladin goes back to Syria to teach Nuradin's son, Al-Saleh, to be a good ruler. ☐

h The Caliph tells Yusuf to kill Shawar. ☐

i Yusuf changes his name to Saladin because he wants to be a good Muslim. ☐

j Many Syrians are afraid of Saladin, and they fight him, but his army wins. ☐

The Citadel in Aleppo is one of the oldest and largest castles in the world. Most of the buildings that you can see today were built by Saladin and his son, Al-Zahir Al-Ghazi.

WORD WORK

Correct the highlighted words in these sentences. They are all new words from Chapter 4.

a Yusuf was the new commentator of the Egyptian army.   ..commander..

b Amalric and his knights attached the Syrians again, but they lost.   ....

c The emirs wanted to rude Syria in the name of Nuradin's son.   ....

d Saladin's men were royal to him.   ....

e Nuradin didn't must Saladin and wanted him to go back to Syria.   ....

f The Muslims and the Franks followed different regions.   ....

g 'We must pay to God to help us,' he said.   ....

h People said that the Assassins' general had secret flowers.   ....

i Yusuf and Shirkuh always followed Nuradin's borders.   ....

j Yusuf's uncle taught him how to organic large armies.   ....

k Saladin made a train to catch people who went into his room.   ....

GUESS WHAT

What does Saladin do in the next chapter? Tick one box.

a He kills King Baldwin. ☐

b He attacks the Frankish army in Palestine. ☐

c He marries a Frankish princess. ☐

d He takes Jerusalem from the Franks. ☐

Chapter 5 – Defeat and victory

Saladin's army marched out of Cairo singing war songs. A young soldier riding beside Saladin asked, 'Why do the Franks hold Jerusalem when it's so holy for us Muslims?'

'It's a very long story,' said Saladin:

*The problem is that the city of Jerusalem is holy for the Franks too. Jesus lived much of his life in the city, and also died there. Jerusalem is the most important place of pilgrimage for people from Europe, but when the Turks took it in 1071, it was more difficult for Europeans to visit. They were angry about that and they decided that they wanted Jerusalem back. They called their campaign a **crusade**. They came from across the sea and in 1099 they took the holy city. They killed nearly everyone in the place! Now, after almost a hundred years, many Franks are born in Palestine and they think that it's their home.*

*Of course, as you know, Jerusalem is a holy place for Muslims, too, because the Prophet Mohammed, **peace** be on him, travelled from there up into the sky to meet God and the prophets. Also the Al-Aqsa **Mosque** is one of the oldest holy places of Islam. It's wrong that the Franks are using the building as a church and praying in it. Nuradin wanted to bring Muslims together to win it back, and I want to make his great hope come true!*

Planning this new campaign, Saladin remembered Shirkuh saying, 'Never waste time. March quickly and take the enemy by surprise!' At first, Saladin's soldiers followed his orders. They were fast and deadly. The Frankish knights weren't ready, and the Muslims won without trying very hard. But then Saladin's men slowed down and stopped being careful. They thought that they could take Jerusalem without any trouble!

King Baldwin the Leper was only sixteen when he learned that Saladin's army was attacking Palestine, and that there was no

crusade a holy war

peace quiet times; a time when there is no war

mosque Muslims go here to pray

one to stop them. He called all his knights together from their castles with letters that his soldiers carried secretly through the Muslim army lines. It was a dangerous plan, but it worked. The Franks arrived to help their king and they surprised Saladin's army at Ramla. Saladin's soldiers had to run to escape and the Franks nearly killed Saladin. It was a very bad **defeat,** and after it many emirs no longer wanted to be in Saladin's army.

Saladin told his men, 'Thinking that Baldwin the Leper is weak because he's young and ill was a mistake! We'll have to work harder to take Jerusalem. Some of you must ride the fastest **camels** to Cairo to tell the Egyptians that we're safe. We've lost a battle, but we can win the war if we fight together!'

The only good news for Saladin was that, after Ramla, Baldwin's army wasn't ready to keep fighting. 'But we must do something to stop him,' Baldwin said to his knights. 'Make all your castles strong and next time we'll be ready for the enemy!'

defeat when an army loses

camel a large animal that people use for travelling across very dry country

The knights decided to build a new castle on the Jordan River. King Baldwin said, 'Don't build at Jacob's **Ford**! Franks and Muslims live on both sides of the river and everyone can cross the Jordan freely there. We'll have trouble if we change things.'

But the knights didn't listen and built the castle there, and in 1179 there was a fight about the land. During the battle, a small group of Saladin's soldiers nearly caught King Baldwin. Old Humphrey of Toron helped his king escape, but the knight was badly wounded and died. Saladin, now forty-one, was sad. 'Humphrey was my good friend in Alexandria after that terrible siege finished. He was a chivalrous man and a brave knight. I wish that more Franks could be like him!'

After the battle of Jacob's Ford, Saladin sent his army in small groups to attack Palestine. 'It'll be easy to catch Saladin's men when they come back,' Baldwin said. 'They'll be tired and we can fight small groups of soldiers and win!' Near the Litani River, they met some of Saladin's men on their way home. Baldwin's knights quickly won the battle, but before they knew it, Saladin and the rest of his army arrived. Saladin's soldiers killed hundreds of Franks, and caught many of their important knights.

Three years later, Baldwin and Saladin agreed to stop fighting for a while, but the peace was short. One of Baldwin's knights, Reynald of Chatillon, was a man who was hungry for gold and for power. When he married, his wife gave him Kerak Castle which looked down on the road that ran between Damascus and Makkah. This castle made it easy for him to attack Muslim pilgrims and to take their money from them.

'Reynald, you are breaking the peace,' King Baldwin told him angrily. 'We have promised the Muslims that the pilgrims' road will be safe.'

ford a place where a river is not deep and you can walk across it

'Your promise doesn't worry me. Anyone crossing my land must pay!' said Reynald.

Saladin thought that Reynald was a man without **honour**, and he decided to stop him. He marched to Kerak with his men. But when Saladin was just going to attack the castle with siege engines, he heard that Isabella of Jerusalem was marrying the grandson of his old friend, Humphrey of Toron, there. 'Find out where the party will be,' he said to his soldiers, 'I don't want to hit that side of the building!' To thank Saladin for this, Isabella sent food to the men in his army.

Later, King Baldwin went to help Reynald. Together they ended the siege and pushed Saladin and his army back. After this, Reynald went on attacking Muslim pilgrims.

'We must stop Reynald and the Franks,' Saladin said to his generals, 'But we must make them fight in open country. They're too strong in their castles!'

honour a man of honour keeps his word and always does the right thing

35

READING CHECK

Choose the right words to finish the sentences.

a At first Saladin's army ...
  1 ☑ were fast and won many battles.
  2 ☐ were slow and weren't careful.
  3 ☐ thought that Baldwin was a strong king.

b King Baldwin called his knights to fight ...
  1 ☐ by using men on camels.
  2 ☐ by marching quickly.
  3 ☐ by sending letters through Muslim army lines.

c At Ramla, Baldwin and the Franks ...
  1 ☐ were taken by surprise.
  2 ☐ nearly killed Saladin.
  3 ☐ didn't want to fight Saladin.

d ... build a new castle at Jacob's Ford.
  1 ☐ Baldwin told his knights to ...
  2 ☐ Saladin's army wanted to ...
  3 ☐ Baldwin didn't want his knights to ...

e At the battle of Jacob's Ford ...
  1 ☐ King Baldwin was caught by Saladin's soldiers.
  2 ☐ a good knight was wounded and died.
  3 ☐ Saladin's soldiers killed hundreds of Franks.

f After three years at war, Baldwin and Saladin ...
  1 ☐ agreed to stop fighting.
  2 ☐ decided to rule Palestine together.
  3 ☐ fought their last battle.

g The peace was broken by ...
  1 ☐ pilgrims travelling from Damascus to Makkah.
  2 ☐ one of Baldwin's knights, Reynald of Chatillon.
  3 ☐ some of Saladin's soldiers.

h Saladin goes to attack Kerak castle because ...
  1 ☐ Isabella of Jerusalem is there.
  2 ☐ he wants to hurt Humphrey of Toron's grandson.
  3 ☐ Reynald of Chatillon lives there.

WORD WORK

Use the words in the picture to complete the sentences.

crusades defeat honour mosque ford peace

a He was a good man, and he fought with great ..honour.. , never losing a battle.

b The knight left his home, and he went on one of the .... to Palestine.

c You must take off your shoes before you visit the ....

d You can't cross the river here, but there's a .... in the next village.

e After their .... in the battle, the army went home sadly.

f After they agreed to stop fighting, there was .... in the country.

GUESS WHAT

What happens in the next chapter? Tick the boxes.

a Saladin …

   1 ☐ wins some important battles against the Franks.

   2 ☐ doesn't want to take Jerusalem.

b King Baldwin …

   1 ☐ becomes weaker and weaker and then dies.

   2 ☐ wins against Saladin in a terrible battle.

c Reynald of Chatillon …

   1 ☐ becomes King of the Franks.

   2 ☐ loses against Saladin, and his head is cut off.

Chapter 6 – A great general

After Nuradin's son Al-Saleh died in 1181, Syria and Egypt could fight fully on the same side at last. At the same time, the Franks had terrible problems. King Baldwin's leprosy made him weak; he couldn't see, and he couldn't fight. It was hard for him to be King of Jerusalem and he had no son. Two people wanted to take his place and be King of the Franks. One was Raymond of Tripoli. He spoke Arabic and he understood both Muslims and Franks well. But there was another knight, new in the Holy Land – Guy of Lusignan. He arrived from Europe and married King Baldwin's sister. When Baldwin died in 1184, the Franks made Guy King of the Franks, because they thought that Raymond was too friendly with the Muslims.

In 1187, Saladin, now forty-nine, spoke to his generals:

'The Franks' new king is weak, but they are still brave and, when they fight together, their armour and their big horses make them very strong. Our horses are smaller, but faster. We wear less armour, but we move more quickly. We're better at fighting in the desert. We're also much faster at sending news to each other with carrier pigeons. We must be clever if we're going to win against them, so I have a plan. We'll attack Raymond of Tripoli's castle near Lake Tiberias and my hope is that they'll hurry to fight us, forgetting the problems of moving a large army over that part of the country.'

When the Franks heard that Saladin's army was at Tiberias, many of them wanted to march at once, but Raymond said, 'Tiberias belongs to me. I've never seen so strong a Muslim army, and I think that we're not wise to fight them even if my castle and my wife are in danger!'

carrier pigeons special birds that carry letters

But Reynald of Chatillon replied, 'You're trying to make us afraid because you prefer the Muslims to us!'

Raymond then said, 'I'm one of you. I'll do what you wish and fight at your side, but you'll see what happens.'

◇◇◇◇◇◇◇◇◇◇◇◇◇◇◇◇◇◇◇◇

In early July, Saladin was waiting by the lake. He took time to look carefully to find the best place to fight. The Frankish army left from Saffuriya. It was only about four hours' journey for a man on a horse to get from there to Lake Tiberias, but moving an army with foot soldiers and knights in heavy armour under the hot summer sun was difficult. There was no water on the dry road and men and horses were very thirsty. Saladin's men spent the whole day attacking the slowly moving soldiers, shooting arrows at them to make them travel even more slowly. The Franks wanted to get to the lake before evening, but they only got to Hattin. There they had to stop. Looking down the hill, they saw Saladin's army waiting by the lake. They couldn't

get to the water, and no man or horse in the Frankish army had anything to drink all through the night.

Next morning, Frankish foot soldiers ran to get water, but many died under the swords and arrows of the Muslim army.

Then Saladin told his men to light fires in the dry grass in front of the Frankish army. Smoke filled the Franks' eyes and mouths. They couldn't see the enemy, but still they fought. Twelve hundred knights left the day before from Saffuriya. Only one hundred and fifty knights were alive when Saladin's seventeen-year-old son Al-Afdal described what he saw that day:

*Hattin was my first battle and I was at my father's side. In the end, the King of the Franks was on the hill. He and his soldiers made an attack that drove our men back to where my father and I were standing. My father cried, 'They mustn't win!' and our men attacked the hill again. I was happy when I saw the Franks fall back. I cried, 'We've won!' But the Franks attacked again with all their **strength** and our men were all around us again. Then my father told them to attack once more, and they pushed the enemy up the hill another time. Again I screamed, 'We've beaten them!' But my father turned to me and said, 'Be silent! We'll win only when that red **tent** on the hill falls!' Before he finished his words, the king's tent fell. My father then got off his horse, **bowed** down and thanked God, crying happily.*

strength being strong

tent a kind of house made of cloth that you can take with you when you move

bow to put down your head in front of someone important

agreement a plan that two or more people or countries have agreed together

After the battle, Saladin's men took King Guy and Reynald of Chatillon to their commander's tent. Saladin asked both of them to sit. He then said to Reynald, 'How many promises and **agreements** have you broken?'

Reynald answered, 'Kings have always done things in this way! I did nothing more.'

King Guy was very thirsty and afraid. Saladin spoke to him kindly and gave him cold water. The king drank and then gave some water to Reynald.

Saladin said, 'You gave him water, not I. He isn't my guest so I don't have to be **merciful** to him!' Then he took his sword and cut off Reynald's head. Guy was afraid, but Saladin said to him, 'True kings don't kill each other!'

After Hattin, Saladin spoke to his generals, 'Many of you will think that it is time to go home to rest. We've won a great victory, but we can't stop fighting now. We must take all the towns and the land that the Franks hold in Palestine!'

They went on attacking Raymond's castle at Tiberias. His wife fought bravely, but she had only a few men to help her. In the end, she surrendered. Saladin let her leave the castle safely with her children. By September, the Muslim army held the towns of Acre, Nablus, Jaffa, Toron, Sidon, Beirut, and Ascalon. Only Tyre still fought against Saladin, but he decided that his men were really tired and could not go on with the siege there. 'It's better for us to take Jerusalem,' he said to his generals, 'But I don't want to be like the Franks all those years ago, killing everyone. Let's see what we can do.'

merciful showing kindness to someone and not hurting them

ACTIVITIES

READING CHECK

Match the two parts of the sentences to summarize Chapter 6.

a After Nuradin's son dies,

b King Baldwin becomes weak and dies

c Two knights want

d The Franks make Guy of Lusignan king

e Saladin plans a battle at Lake Tiberias

f The Franks lose the battle at Hattin

g King Guy and Reynald of Chatillon

h Saladin saves King Guy

i Saladin decides that it's time

1 because it's hard to move a large Frankish army across the desert.

2 for his army to take Jerusalem.

3 to be the new King of the Franks.

4 Syria and Egypt fight on the same side.

5 because they have no water.

6 but he kills Reynald of Chatillon.

7 because he isn't friendly with the Muslims.

8 without leaving a son.

9 meet Saladin after the battle.

WORD WORK

Complete the sentences with new words from Chapter 6.

This exercise builds up your s _ _ _ _ _ _ _ .

The generals came to an a _ _ _ _ _ _ _ _ .

They used c _ _ _ _ _ _ p _ _ _ _ _ _ to take messages.

We're sleeping in t _ _ _ _ tonight.

He b _ _ _ _ when he met the queen.

'Please be m _ _ _ _ _ _ _ with me!'

GUESS WHAT

Who do you read about in the next chapter? Tick three pictures.

a Turan Shah,
Saladin's brother

b Al-Afdal,
Saladin's son

c Balian of Ibelin,
a Frankish knight

d Nuradin

e King Guy

Chapter 7 – The City of God

patriarch the most important man in the Frankish Church in Palestine

mount mountain

rubbish things that you do not want any more

bury to put a dead body under the ground

'I want to be like Caliph Umar,' said Saladin to his men:

When his armies won all of Palestine in the early days of Islam, he took Jerusalem peacefully and entered the town like a poor man, on foot. The **Patriarch** *Sophronius gave him the keys of the town after they made a peace agreement. It said that the Franks, their houses and churches were safe, and that they could pray in the way they wanted, and that no Muslim was going to hurt them or take their money. Then Umar visited the town with the Patriarch. When he saw that people used the Holy* **Mount** *in the middle of the town as a place for* **rubbish***, he started to clean it with his own hands. Then he asked men to build what is now the Al-Aqsa Mosque there. After that, when he went with the Patriarch to see the church where they* **buried** *Jesus, it was time to pray. Umar left the church to pray outside. He said, 'If I pray inside the church, then one day other Muslims will want to make it into a mosque!' He was generous to all religions.*

'We agree that we don't want to hurt people in the town. But the Franks fight to the last man!' Saladin's generals said.

When Saladin met the Franks, he said, 'I think – like you – that Jerusalem is the City of God. I don't want to attack God's home. So, if you surrender, then you will all be free to leave it with your things. Your churches will be safe, and when people want to make a pilgrimage to the holy places, they can travel freely into the town at any time.'

The Franks knew that they weren't strong, but they said, 'How can we give you the town where Jesus died? If we let you take Jerusalem without fighting, people will rightly say that we're afraid to die for Jesus. We must do our best to hold it!'

'Then I'll take Jerusalem by the sword, and many people will lose their lives!' Saladin promised.

◇◇◇◇◇◇◇◇◇◇◇◇◇◇◇◇◇◇◇

The Franks' commander was Balian of Ibelin, one of the very best of the Frankish knights. He fought bravely at Hattin, and after he escaped from the battle, he went to Saladin. He asked the Muslim commander, 'Can I take my wife and children out of Jerusalem to Tyre where they will be safe? I promise that I'll never carry my sword against you again, and that I'll only stay one night in the town.'

Saladin said, 'I'm sure that you're worried about your wife in these difficult times. Go at once and get her. I know that you'll keep your promise not to fight my men.'

But when Balian arrived in Jerusalem, all the people there said, 'You must stay here and be our commander. How can we fight the Muslims without someone to tell us what to do?'

'I can't! I gave my word to Saladin that I wouldn't fight against him. I can't break my promise,' Balian replied.

The men of the church said that it wasn't wrong to break a promise to a Muslim, but Balian was a man of honour. He wrote to Saladin and said:

The people of Jerusalem have asked for my help as their commander. What shall I do?

tears the water that comes from your eye when you cry

Saladin answered at once:

> *You must help your people. Forget your promise to me. And don't worry about your wife and children. I know that you cannot take care of them now. Fifty of my best men will take them safely to Tyre!*

Tears came to Balian's eyes when he read Saladin's answer. He thought, 'Why aren't our people as good as Saladin?'

Balian did his best to make the town ready for the siege, but there were only two other knights to help him.

He said, 'This city is full of people running away from the other towns in Palestine that the Muslims have taken. Most of

you are women and children, but I'm going to make every man here over sixteen into a knight, and we'll do our best to fight for Jesus and Jerusalem!'

The siege began, and at first the Franks held the city. But after a few days, Saladin moved his army and all his siege engines to attack the town's walls from the Mount of **Olives**. Muslim arrows made the blue sky as black as night, and fell like rain on the Franks. Worse was 'Greek fire', a terrible weapon that Saladin's soldiers shot from their siege engines. It lit fires at once on anything that it hit, and so the town began to burn, and the city walls began to fall. The Franks prayed for God's help in their churches, and mothers cut their daughters' hair very short in the hope of making them ugly, to keep them safe from the soldiers. People remembered what happened when the Franks took the town one hundred years before. They couldn't stop thinking about how many people died then.

Patriarch Heraclius not only worried about the people, but also about all the holy things and the gold in the churches. He told Balian, 'Go and see Saladin. He's always generous.'

'My men are already on the walls!' the Muslim commander told Balian when he came to talk, 'You said that you wanted to fight, so the time to be merciful is over!'

Balian answered, 'Many of the people are not fighting very hard in the hope that you will be generous with us as you have been with other towns in Palestine. But we soldiers, when we see that a fight to the death is the only way, we'll come out and fight you and we'll die for God. We'll take as many of your men as we can with us, or we'll win with honour!'

Saladin liked Balian's brave words so he turned to his generals and the **imams** and said, 'What must I do? I promised to take the town by the sword, and I can't break my word!'

olive a tree that has small green or black fruits with a salty taste

imam this man helps Muslims to pray in a mosque

READING CHECK

1 Put these sentences in the correct order to summarize Chapter 7.

a ☐ In Jerusalem the people ask Balian to be their commander.

b ☐ The Muslims begin the siege of Jerusalem.

c ☐ Saladin meets the Franks and asks them to surrender.

d ☐ Balian writes a letter to Saladin.

e ☐ Saladin asks his generals and imams if they should go on fighting.

f ☐ Balian goes to Jerusalem to rescue his wife and children.

g ☐ Saladin's soldiers take Balian's wife and children to Tyre.

h ☐ Patriarch Heraclius sends Balian to talk to Saladin.

i ☐ Balian prepares the city to fight Saladin's army.

2 What do they say?

❶ Can I take my wife and children out of Jerusalem?

❷ You said that you wanted to fight. The time to be merciful is over.

❸ I want to be like Caliph Umar.

❹ How can we give you the town where Jesus died?

❺ If you surrender, you will all be free to leave.

❻ You must stay here and be our commander.

a Saladin tells his men: ③

b Saladin tells the Franks in Jerusalem: ☐

c The Franks say to Saladin: ☐

d Balian asks Saladin: ☐

e The people of Jerusalem tell Balian: ☐

f Saladin tells Balian: ☐

WORD WORK

Complete the crossword.

ACROSS

2 When you cry, these come from your eyes.

3 To put a dead body under the ground.

4 He helps Muslims to pray in a mosque.

7 Things that you don't want any more.

DOWN

1 He was the most important man in the Frankish Church in Palestine.

5 Another word for 'mountain'.

6 A tree that has small black or green fruits.

GUESS WHAT

What happens in the last chapter? Are these sentences true or false? Tick the boxes.

	True	False
a Saladin's soldiers kill all the Franks in Jerusalem.	☐	☐
b The rich Franks have to pay to leave the city.	☐	☐
c Balian and Saladin help the poor people.	☐	☐
d King Guy goes free, but he breaks his promise to Saladin.	☐	☐
e The Europeans organize a new crusade to Palestine.	☐	☐
f Saladin dies in a battle with King Richard.	☐	☐
g There is no money to pay for Saladin's funeral.	☐	☐

Chapter 8 – A man of honour

'We must save the holy places!' went on Saladin.

But the imams said to him, 'The Franks will be our prisoners. To be free, they must pay a **ransom**: ten gold pieces for a man, five gold pieces for a woman, and one gold piece for a child. They'll have forty days to find the money. It's the only way that we can pay for the war!'

Saladin spoke to Balian. 'Our soldiers will watch the streets to stop criminals hurting people and stealing things,' he said. 'Churches will be safe, and people can come on pilgrimage here when they want.'

Balian answered, 'You're very generous, but I'm worried about the poor. I'll pay for as many poor people as I can to go free.'

When Saladin's brother Al-Adil heard this, he said, 'I want to help too! I'll pay the ransom for a thousand poor people!'

Saladin said, 'I have another good **idea**! Old people and men with young children can go free too. Also, many women have lost their husbands in the fighting, and many children are without mothers or fathers. To all of these I want to give money.'

Saladin's **treasurers** were worried. 'If all these people can leave freely, how will we pay our soldiers? We must ask the rich people to give more!' they said.

ransom the money that people must pay to be free after their enemy catches them

idea a plan or a thought

treasurer this person keeps money for a king or group of people

When the Patriarch left with all the gold from the churches, many Muslims were angry, but Saladin said, 'We won Jerusalem to give the city back to God and to Islam, not to be rich!'

But Saladin's work wasn't over. Tyre was still in the hands of the Franks, who came from all over Palestine when their home towns fell. Now they were ready to fight from Tyre to get their land back. Some of Saladin's generals said, 'We're afraid that the Franks will get help from their friends in Europe.'

But Saladin answered, 'If they come from across the sea, they'll be far from home and they won't win.'

◇◇◇◇◇◇◇◇◇◇◇◇◇◇◇◇◇◇◇

In 1188 Saladin, now fifty, said that King Guy could go free if he promised never to fight the Muslims again. But Guy broke his promise in 1189 and attacked Acre, beginning a long and terrible siege. By then there were many more European knights in Palestine. After the fall of Jerusalem, the Franks told European kings that they needed help to win back the Holy Land. Many answered the call for a new crusade.

In 1191, the King of France arrived in the Holy Land, and two months later Richard, King of England, came too. The Muslims knew that King Richard was brave and strong.

Acre was a dirty town, and King Richard was ill the minute he arrived, but he went on telling his men what to do from his bed. He was a good commander and the town, already in great trouble after two years of endless war, couldn't fight any more. People were dying of hunger because the Franks had the town under siege, and they stopped all food getting into it by land or by sea. Richard told his men to make better siege engines and

the new attacks from these never stopped. The falling stones killed twelve men at a time, and the Muslim generals knew that this was the end.

They sent a letter to Saladin saying that they couldn't fight any longer. Saladin thought that one last fight could win the day. He asked all of his men to attack, but the emirs said, 'We can't win now. There are too many Franks.'

In July 1191, the town surrendered. Saladin asked King Richard to treat his Muslim prisoners well, but the English king wanted to win back other towns in Palestine that the Muslims held. Most of all he wanted Jerusalem, so all Richard's prisoners – Muslim soldiers of Acre, their wives and their children – died under the swords of the Frankish knights that day.

The Franks now marched towards Jerusalem, but it was summer and it was hot. They tried to stay near their ships which were sailing down the **coast**. But Saladin's men never stopped attacking them. Richard's men were brave and they went on, but the army could march only five miles a day. At Arsuf the Franks won a small battle, but the war wasn't over.

The next year saw a lot of fighting, but no real victory for either army. Saladin knew that time was on his side. Richard needed to go home. In the end, they agreed to stop fighting. The Franks kept the land between Tyre and Jaffa, but Saladin kept Jerusalem and the other towns in Palestine that he held. European pilgrims could visit the holy city without danger, and many European knights travelled there to pray, but Richard never went. He left for England without ever seeing Jerusalem.

◇◇◇◇◇◇◇◇◇◇◇◇◇◇◇◇◇◇◇

These last years were difficult for Saladin. After Acre, his emirs were not as happy to fight as before, and it was hard to keep his army together. He was fifty-five years old now, and often

coast the place where the land is next to the sea

ill and tired. 'I wish I could go to Makkah,' he said, but he was now very weak and could not make that long journey. 'At least I can still meet travellers to Makkah when they come home,' he said to himself. He rode out of Damascus early in 1193 to meet a group of pilgrims coming back from Makkah, but the cold weather that day made him ill. Forty-eight hours later he was dead. When they went to bury him, they found that there was no money to pay for his **funeral**. He was always so kind and generous to others, and in the end he left nothing for himself. Many people **mourned** his death at the time, and people everywhere still know of Saladin to this day. We remember him not only as a great general, but also as a good man who was merciful, wise and generous.

funeral the time when a dead person's body is put under the ground

mourn to be sad because someone has died

READING CHECK

Correct ten more mistakes in the story.

doesn't want

Saladin ~~wants~~ to kill the people of Jerusalem but the <u>patriarchs</u> want the Franks to pay to go free. Balian says that he'll pay for some <u>rich</u> people and Saladin and his <u>father</u> agree to help too.

Tyre is still in the hands of the <u>Muslims</u>. Many knights travel there from Europe, and then they attack the Muslim city of Acre. When the Kings of France and <u>Germany</u> arrive with their soldiers, Saladin surrenders. But King Richard isn't merciful, and he <u>saves</u> all the Muslim soldiers and their families.

The Franks then try to win back <u>Cairo</u>, but the fighting goes on for a long time. In the end King Richard and <u>Balian</u> make a peace agreement, and Richard goes back to England.

Saladin is old and ill. He wants to go to <u>England</u>, but he can't travel. One day he goes out to meet some pilgrims, gets ill, and dies. There's no money to pay for the <u>hospital</u> because he's given it all away.

ACTIVITIES

WORD WORK

1 Find new words from Chapter 8.

a tacos

b refalun

c aide

d ronum

e smoarn

f strearure

a c o a s t
b f _ _ _ _ _ _
c i _ _ _
d m _ _ _ _
e r _ _ _ _ _
f t _ _ _ _ _ _ _ _

2 Complete the sentences with the words in Activity 1 in the correct form.

a The house is on the ...coast..., only two minutes from the sea.

b Your .... for stories are really good.

c They paid a big .... before the man went free.

d The king's .... was worried about how to pay the soldiers.

e My grandfather has died and we're having his .... today.

f She's still .... the death of her husband, who died last year.

WHAT NEXT?

Find out more about Saladin. Then cross out two false sentences.

a Saladin had seventeen sons.

b Three of his sons became the rulers of Damascus, Egypt, and Aleppo after he died.

c Saladin's family ruled for five hundred and seventy years after his death.

d King Richard died and his brother, John, was the next king of England.

e There is nothing left today of the city walls that Saladin built in Cairo.

f There have been Egyptian, American, and Swedish films about Saladin.

g A 2009 TV cartoon series about Saladin was made in Malaysia.

h Saladin's campaigns are part of the computer game *Age of Empires II*.

Project A *A holiday postcard from a city*

1 Read the holiday postcard from Cairo and match the days with the sights.

Monday   Tuesday   Wednesday   Thursday   Friday

Dear Miranda,

Having a great time in Cairo. Arrived yesterday (Monday). Staying at hotel in Heliopolis. Visited Khan el-Khalili market yesterday. Today will go to see pyramids and sphinx in Giza. Tomorrow hope to visit Sultan Hassan Mosque and see mummies in Egyptian Museum. Want to see Citadel too before I come home Friday. See you soon.

Love and best wishes,

Lily

a Citadel ....

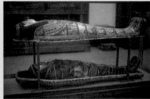

b Egyptian Museum ....

c Khan el-Khalili market ....

d pyramids ....

e Sultan Hassan Mosque ....

f sphinx ....

2 **In postcards we often miss out small words (pronouns, auxiliary verbs, articles, prepositions). Cross out the words we can miss out in these sentences.**

   a We're having a wonderful time in Damascus.

   b I'm staying at a hotel in Sultanahmet.

   c We visited the Ommayyad Mosque yesterday.

   d I'm going to relax in the Ein Gedi spa at the Dead Sea today.

   e Tomorrow we hope to go swimming in the Red Sea.

   f The day after tomorrow I will go to the Mount of Olives.

   g I want to see the Mehter band in the Army Museum on Thursday.

   h I'm planning to spend a day in Petra too before I leave.

3 **Choose another city and write a holiday postcard from there. Don't forget to miss out small words.**

Ommayad Mosque

Mehter band

diving in Red Sea

Mount of Olives

Project B *A famous army commander*

1 Look at the encyclopedia text about Saladin and complete the table below.

Saladin, Arabic *Salah ad-Din,* 1138–1193, Muslim soldier and ruler of Egypt, Syria, and Jerusalem, born in Tikrit, Mesopotamia. His father was Ayyub, governor of Tikrit. He lived for 10 years in Damascus at ruler Nuradin's court, where he learnt about Muslim law. He went with his uncle, Shirkuh, one of Nuradin's generals, on campaigns (1164, 1167) against the Fatimid rulers of Egypt. On Shirkuh's death (1169) Saladin became Vizier of Egypt. After Nuradin's death, Saladin ruled Egypt and Damascus, and fought against the Frankish Kings of Jerusalem. Saladin won his most famous battle – the battle of Hattin – in 1187 and took Jerusalem. Saladin fought against Richard I of England in the Third Crusade (1189–1192). In 1192, Saladin made peace with the Crusaders. The Franks were left the lands between Acre and Jaffa on the coast. Saladin died in Damascus in 1193 of a fever. We remember him today for being a generous, chivalrous man of honour, and for winning back Jerusalem from the Franks.

When was he born?	
Where was he born?	
Who was his father?	
What did he learn about when he was young?	
Who did he fight against?	
Which lands did he rule?	
What was his most famous battle?	
When, where, and how did he die?	
Why do we remember him?	

2 Complete the text about Alexander the Great using information from the table.

Alexander the Great, *Mégas Aléxandros*, ... BCE-............... BCE, King of Macedon and ruler of .... , Egypt, Cyprus, ... , and India, born in .... , the capital of .... , to King .... and his wife .... When he was young, he lived at his father's court, where Aristotle taught him .... On Philip's death (336 BCE) Alexander became Alexander III of Macedon. He was twenty. In 334 BCE Alexander took his army east and began a campaign against .... , the King of .... In November 333 BCE the Persians lost to Alexander at his most famous battle – the Battle of .... in South Anatolia. Alexander died of a .... in .... He had three wives, and two sons – ...., and .... – who both died young. We remember Alexander today for naming the city of .... in Egypt after himself, and bringing .... to different countries. He is famous too for being .... and for ....

When was he born?	*356 BCE*
Where was he born?	*Pellas, capital of Macedon*
Who were his father and mother?	*Philip II and Olympias*
What did he learn when he was young?	*Greek philosophy*
Who did he fight against?	*King Darius III of Persia*
Which lands did he rule?	*Macedon, Greece, Egypt, Cyprus, Persia, India*
What was his most famous battle?	*the Battle of Issus*
How, where, and when did he die?	*of a fever in Babylon, in 323 BCE*
How many children did he have?	*two – Herakles, and Alexander IV*
Why do we remember him?	*for naming Alexandria in Egypt; bringing Greek ways to different countries; being a great army commander, and dying young.*

Project B   *A famous army commander*

3   **Find out about another famous army commander. Write a text about your chosen commander. Use the texts in exercise 1 and 2 to help you.**

Hannibal

Napoleon

George Patton

Julius Caesar

GRAMMAR CHECK

Past Continuous: affirmative and negative

We use the Past Continuous to talk about longer actions in the past. To make the Past Continuous affirmative, we use was/were + the –ing form of the verb.

A soldier was holding a knife to a woman's neck.

To make the Past Continuous negative, we use wasn't/weren't + the –ing form of the verb.

He wasn't thinking when he killed the man.

When a verb ends in a consonant + –e, we remove the –e and add –ing.

come – coming ride – riding smile – smiling

When a verb ends in a consonant + vowel + consonant, we double the final consonant and add –ing.

get – getting hit – hitting run – running

1 Complete the sentences. Use the Past Continuous form of the verbs in brackets.

a Ayyub's brother Shirkuh ...*was asking*... (ask) for news.

b The three brothers .... (sit) in the garden of their house in Baalbek.

c They .... (listen) to their father who .... (tell) a story.

d A man .... (run) on the other side of the river.

e The general .... (not smile).

f Many soldiers .... (ride) their horses after him.

g 'Suddenly the soldiers .... (shoot) at us.'

h They .... (not take) the same road to Egypt.

i Lots of arrows .... (hit) the boat.

j Yusuf .... (play) polo.

k The boys .... (read) the holy Koran. They .... (learn) about the Prophet Yusuf.

l The soldiers .... (fight) hard.

GRAMMAR

GRAMMAR CHECK

Verb + infinitive or –ing form verb

Some verbs, such as *decide*, *forget*, *learn*, *need*, *try*, and *want*, are followed by to + infinitive.

He learned to use his sword well.

He tried to understand the law.

Some verbs, such as *finish*, *go*, *like*, *love*, and *stop*, are followed by the –ing form of the verb.

Yusuf liked learning, and he learned quickly.

Saladin's men stopped being careful.

We can use either the infinitive or the –ing form with *begin*.

He began to read the Koran.

He began reading the Koran.

2 Complete these sentences. Use the infinitive or *–ing* form of the verb in brackets.

a At first, Yusuf wanted ...*to go*... (go) back to Damascus.

b He didn't like .... (live) in Aleppo.

c He wanted .... (learn) how to fight with a sword.

d He tried .... (help) people in the castle.

e Nuradin began .... (talk) to Yusuf about different problems.

f Yusuf decided .... (get) into Nuradin's army.

g He needed .... (find) clever ways to win against stronger men.

h He loved .... (play) polo.

i He forgot .... (worry) about things when he was on Aneed's back.

j Ayyub finished .... (tell) his story.

k He wanted .... (show) his uncle that he was a real soldier.

l They began .... (cross) the hot dry land, and a deadly desert storm nearly killed them.

GRAMMAR CHECK

Linkers: so and because

We can use so to link two parts of a sentence talking about the result of something.

Yusuf knew everything about the army so Shirkuh took his nephew with him to Egypt.

(= result of first part of sentence)

We can use because to link two parts of a sentence talking about the reason for something.

It didn't take Yusuf long to get ready because he had only a few things to take with him.

(= reason for first part of sentence)

We can put *because* at the beginning or in the middle of a sentence.

Because Yusuf had only a few things to take with him it didn't take him long to get ready.

3 Complete the sentences with *so* or *because*.

a Yusuf learned a lot in Egypt .....because..... he watched how his uncle fought battles.

b .... the Syrians helped Shawar he became the strongest man in Egypt.

c Shawar didn't want to pay gold to Nuradin .... he asked the Franks to help him.

d Shirkuh travelled through the Sinai Desert .... he wanted to surprise Shawar.

e Shirkuh's men were very weak .... he decided to stop and wait at Giza.

f Most Egyptians didn't like Shawar .... he was friendly with the Franks.

g Yusuf's men turned and ran .... the Franks followed them.

h .... the people of Alexandria were friendly with the Syrians the Franks fought them.

i Humphrey of Toron said that Yusuf was good .... he thought about old people and children.

j Shawar wanted the Syrian army out of Egypt .... he gave them gold.

GRAMMAR CHECK

Comparative and superlative adjectives

To make comparative adjectives, we add **–er to most short adjectives.**

strong – stronger

When adjectives finish in e, we add –r. When they finish in a consonant + y, we change the y to i and add –er. When they finish in a short vowel + consonant, we double the consonant and add –er.

safe – safer   *friendly – friendlier*   *thin – thinner*

With other adjectives with two or more syllables, we put more before the adjective.

careful – more careful

To make superlative adjectives, we use the + add –est or –st to shorter adjectives, or use the + most with longer adjectives.

strong – the strongest   *careful – the most careful*

Some superlative adjectives are irregular:

good – the best   *bad – the worst*

4 Complete the sentence. Use the comparative or superlative form of the adjective in brackets.

a Shirkuh died halfway through
 the most wonderful (wonderful) meal.

b Al-Saleh was two years ....
 (young) than Baldwin.

c It was .... (bad) day that
 people in Bilbais could remember.

d Deciding on the best person to be the next vizier was
 .... (difficult) thing.

e Saladin felt that it was ....
 (important) to help people than to be rich.

f Saladin made the walls of Cairo
 .... (strong) than before.

g Nuradin became .... (angry) with Yusuf after that.

h Saladin needed a .... (big) army to move against the
 Franks.

i Saladin's army was .... (good) than the emirs' army.

GRAMMAR

GRAMMAR CHECK

Imperatives

We use imperatives to give instructions, orders, or invitations, or to make offers. Affirmative imperatives look the same as the infinitive without *to*.

March quickly and take the enemy by surprise!

Negative imperatives start with do not or don't + infinitive without *to*.

Don't build at Jacob's Ford.

We can use (*not*) *ever*, *never* and *always* with imperatives.

Don't ever say that!   *Never waste time!*   *Always do as I say!*

We can use *please* to soften an imperative.

Please listen to me.

5 **Complete the sentences with the affirmative or negative imperative. Use the words in the box.**

> be   don't hit   don't speak   don't take   enjoy
> fight   ~~give~~   make   remember   think

a '....Give.... Jerusalem back to us!' cried the Crusaders.

b 'Always .... careful,' Saladin told his soldiers.

c '............... that the Al-Asqa
mosque is one of the oldest holy
places of Islam,' said Saladin.

d 'Never .... that King
Baldwin is weak,' Saladin told his
men.

e '............... all your castles
strong,' King Baldwin said to his
knights.

f '............... money from Muslim
pilgrims,' said Baldwin to Reynald
de Chatillon.

g '............... to me like that!' said Reynald de Chatillon to the king.

h '............... the side of the castle where they're having their party!' said Saladin.

i 'Please .... the food that I am sending you,' said Isabella to Saladin's soldiers.

j '............... the Franks in open country if you can,' said Saladin to his generals.

GRAMMAR CHECK

Adverbs

We use adverbs to talk about how something is done.

Baldwin's knights quickly won the battle.

Saladin spoke to King Guy kindly.

We make adverbs from adjectives by adding –ly.

nervous – nervously   *impatient – impatiently*

For adjectives that end in consonant + –y, we change the y to i and add –ly.

easy – easily   *happy – happily*

For adjectives that end in consonant + short vowel + short consonant, we double the final consonant.

careful – carefully

Some adverbs are irregular.

fast – fast   *good – well*

6 Write the adverbs.

a angry ..*angrily*..   **e** safe ....

b brave ....   **f** slow ....

c careful ....   **g** thirsty ....

d wise ....   **h** worried ....

7 Complete the sentences. Use the adverbs from activity 6.

a Raymond of Tripoli spoke very ...*wisely*... .

b Saladin looked .... to find the best place to fight.

c The Frankish army moved .... under the hot summer sun.

d The Frankish soldiers looked at the waters of the lake ....

e Saladin .... watched the battle.

f Saladin spoke to Reynald of Chatillon ....

g Raymond's wife fought ....

h She left the castle .... with her children.

GRAMMAR CHECK

Reported speech with say

In direct speech, we give the words that people say.

'I won't fight against you,' said Balian to Saladin.
'We want to fight,' said the Franks in Jerusalem.

In reported speech, we put the verb one step into the past and change the pronouns and possessive adjectives.

Balian said to Saladin that he wouldn't fight against him.
The Franks in Jerusalem said that they wanted to fight.

8 Write the sentences again. Use reported speech.

a 'I want to be like Caliph Umar,' said Saladin.
   Saladin said that he wanted
   to be like Caliph Umar.

b 'If I pray in the church, one day Muslims will want to make it into a mosque,' said Caliph Umar.

   ....

   ....

c 'We don't want to hurt people in the town,' said Saladin's generals.

   ....

   ....

d 'I'll take Jerusalem by the sword, and many people will lose their lives,' said Saladin.

   ....

e 'I'm going to make every man over sixteen into a knight!' said Balian.

   ....

f 'Saladin is always generous,' said Patriarch Heraclius.

   ....

g 'The Franks will be our prisoners,' said the imams.

   ....

h 'We can't win because there are too many Franks,' the emirs said.

   ....

DOMINOES
THE STRUCTURED APPROACH TO READING IN ENGLISH

Dominoes is an enjoyable series of illustrated classic and modern stories in four carefully graded language stages – from Starter to Three – which take learners from beginner to intermediate level.

Each *Domino* reader includes:
- **a good story** to read and enjoy
- **integrated activities** to develop reading skills and increase active vocabulary
- **personalized projects** to make the language and story themes more meaningful
- **seven pages of grammar activities** for consolidation.

Each *Domino* pack contains a reader, plus a MultiROM with:
- **a complete audio recording of the story**, fully dramatized to bring it to life
- **interactive activities** to offer further practice in reading and language skills and to consolidate learning.

If you liked this Level Two *Domino*, why not read these?

The Drive to Dubai
Julie Till

When his father is arrested in Dubai, Kareem has to move fast. He must show that his father is not a thief – and prove that his family is honest. For Kareem is going to marry the beautiful and intelligent Samira Al-Hussein, and she could never marry someone from a bad family.

So Kareem and his brother get to work quickly – with a little help from Samira.

Book ISBN: 978 0 19 424892 1
MultiROM Pack ISBN: 978 0 19 424844 0

The Lost World
Sir Arthur Conan Doyle

'You said that you wanted danger, didn't you?' says McArdle, the editor of the Daily Gazette. And he sends his young reporter, Malone, on a strange journey into South America with the famous Professor Challenger.

Challenger believes that he can find a lost world full of dinosaurs in the middle of the Amazon Forest. But this world is dangerous to reach, and, once the Professor and his small group of explorers arrive, things get even more dangerous for them.

Will they return alive?

Book ISBN: 978 0 19 424880 8
MultiROM Pack ISBN: 978 0 19 424832 7

You can find details and a full list of books in the *Dominoes* catalogue and Oxford English Language Teaching Catalogue, and on the website: www.oup.com/elt

Teachers: see www.oup.com/elt for a full range of online support, or consult your local office.

	CEF	Cambridge Exams	IELTS	TOEFL iBT	TOEIC
Starter	A1	YLE Movers	–	–	–
Level 1	A1–A2	YLE Flyers/KET	3.0	–	–
Level 2	A2–B1	KET-PET	3.0-4.0	–	–
Level 3	B1	PET	4.0	57-86	550